745.5
Tof Tofts, Hannah
Hands-on
do it yourself

DATE DUE

00206

745.5
Tof Tofts, Hannah

AUTHOR

Hands-on

TITLE

Do it yourself

Date Due	BORROWER'S NAME	Grade
APR 10 20	Karen	1A
MAY 03 20	Danielle	KA

00206

HANDS-ON
do-it-yourself

Hannah Tofts

Author: Claire Watts
Photography: Jon Barnes
Cover Photography: James Johnson
Illustration: Kevin Hart

A **TWO-CAN** BOOK
published by
THOMSON LEARNING
New York

Contents

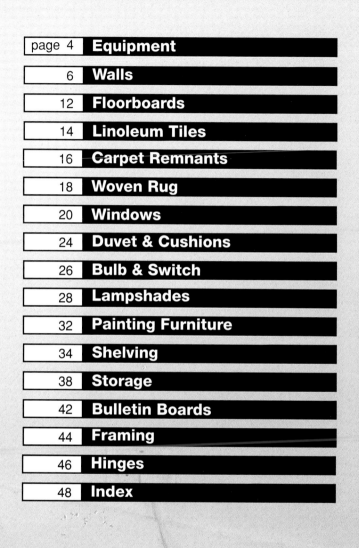

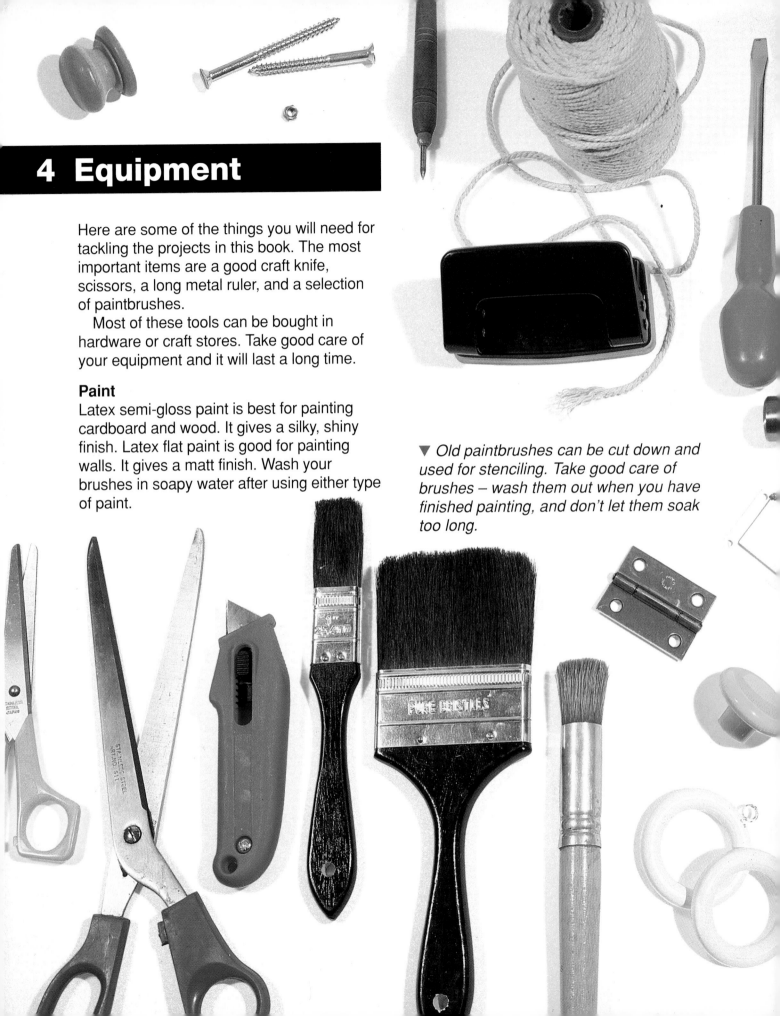

4 Equipment

Here are some of the things you will need for tackling the projects in this book. The most important items are a good craft knife, scissors, a long metal ruler, and a selection of paintbrushes.

Most of these tools can be bought in hardware or craft stores. Take good care of your equipment and it will last a long time.

Paint

Latex semi-gloss paint is best for painting cardboard and wood. It gives a silky, shiny finish. Latex flat paint is good for painting walls. It gives a matt finish. Wash your brushes in soapy water after using either type of paint.

▼ *Old paintbrushes can be cut down and used for stenciling. Take good care of brushes – wash them out when you have finished painting, and don't let them soak too long.*

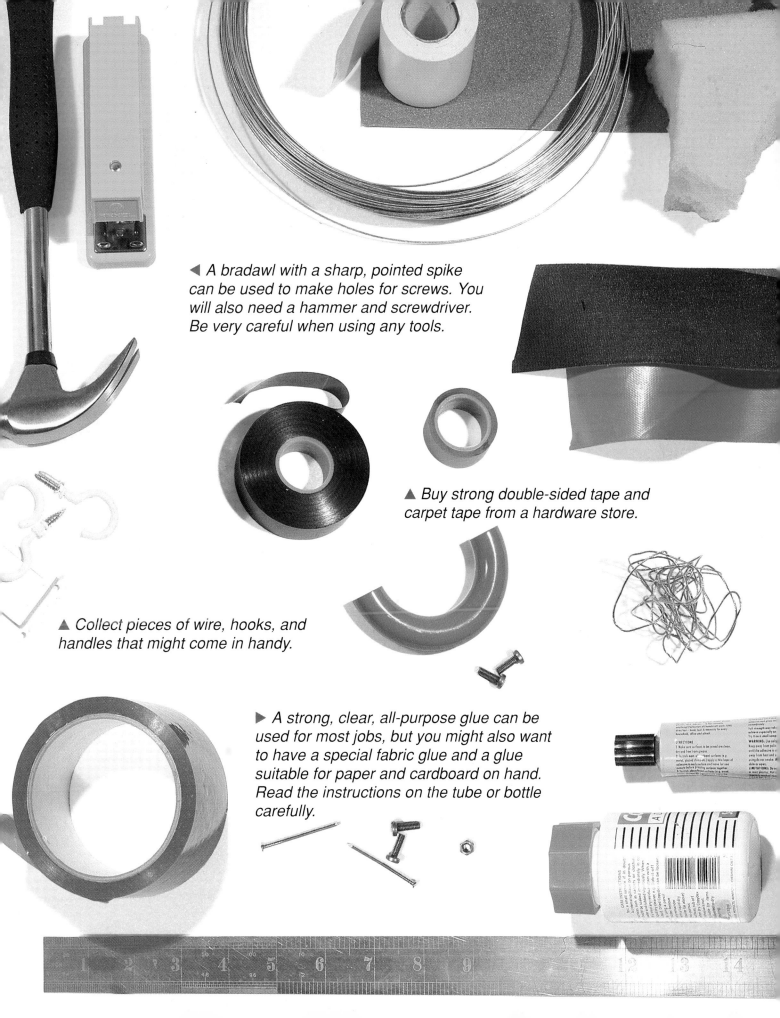

◀ A bradawl with a sharp, pointed spike can be used to make holes for screws. You will also need a hammer and screwdriver. Be very careful when using any tools.

▲ Buy strong double-sided tape and carpet tape from a hardware store.

▲ Collect pieces of wire, hooks, and handles that might come in handy.

▶ A strong, clear, all-purpose glue can be used for most jobs, but you might also want to have a special fabric glue and a glue suitable for paper and cardboard on hand. Read the instructions on the tube or bottle carefully.

6 Walls

Paint the walls of your room with a combination of colors. Choose shades that clash or ones that go well together. Experiment with dark colors on light or light on dark. Try painting over the base coat while it is still wet.

Sponging
First paint a smooth base color, then use a sponge to put another color on top. Try pressing firmly in some places and gently in others.

Ragging
You can create all kinds of effects using a piece of rag. Roll it up into a short, tight roll and use the end to print a pattern; or roll it into a longer shape and use it like a rolling pin.

Paint your molding to coordinate with your walls. Be careful around electrical outlets.

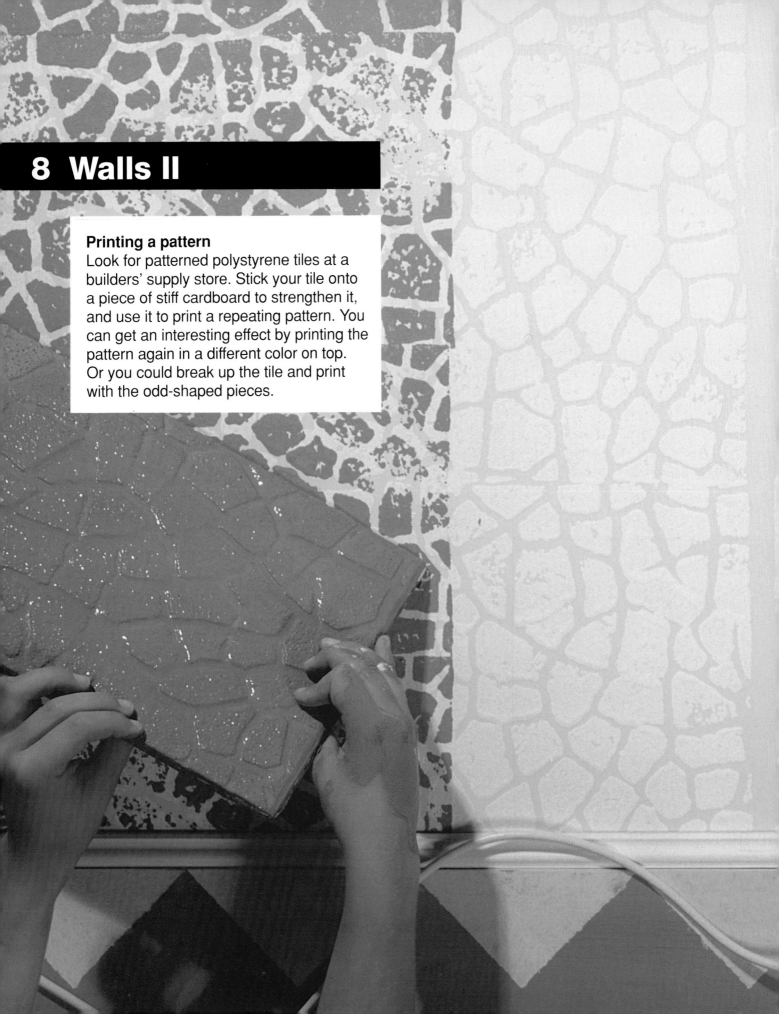

8 Walls II

Printing a pattern
Look for patterned polystyrene tiles at a builders' supply store. Stick your tile onto a piece of stiff cardboard to strengthen it, and use it to print a repeating pattern. You can get an interesting effect by printing the pattern again in a different color on top. Or you could break up the tile and print with the odd-shaped pieces.

Stenciling
It is best to use stencil card, which you can buy from craft stores, because it has a water-resistant surface that makes it durable. Use a craft knife to cut out the shape you want – ask an adult to help. Use a stencil brush with short stiff bristles to stipple the paint over the stencil. It takes a long time to stencil a whole wall, so you might want to start with a simple pattern or a border.

10 Walls III

Painting over

You can make an unusual pattern by painting a contrasting color with light, free strokes over your base coat. Try using paintbrushes of different sizes and experiment with different colors. Make lines by applying the top coat and then dragging a paintbrush firmly through the paint.

Thin paint

If you use a little water to dilute your flat paint, it is easy to make all sorts of patterns in it. Try making wavy stripes using a paintbrush or comb.

Paint over your base coat with watered-down paint and then rub gently with a cloth. You should be able to see the pattern of the brush strokes.

12 Floorboards

If your carpet is wearing thin or you have just moved into a new house, why not paint your floorboards? You could make a design from stencils or paint a rug that looks just like the real thing! If you don't want to paint the whole floor, stencil a border around the edges.

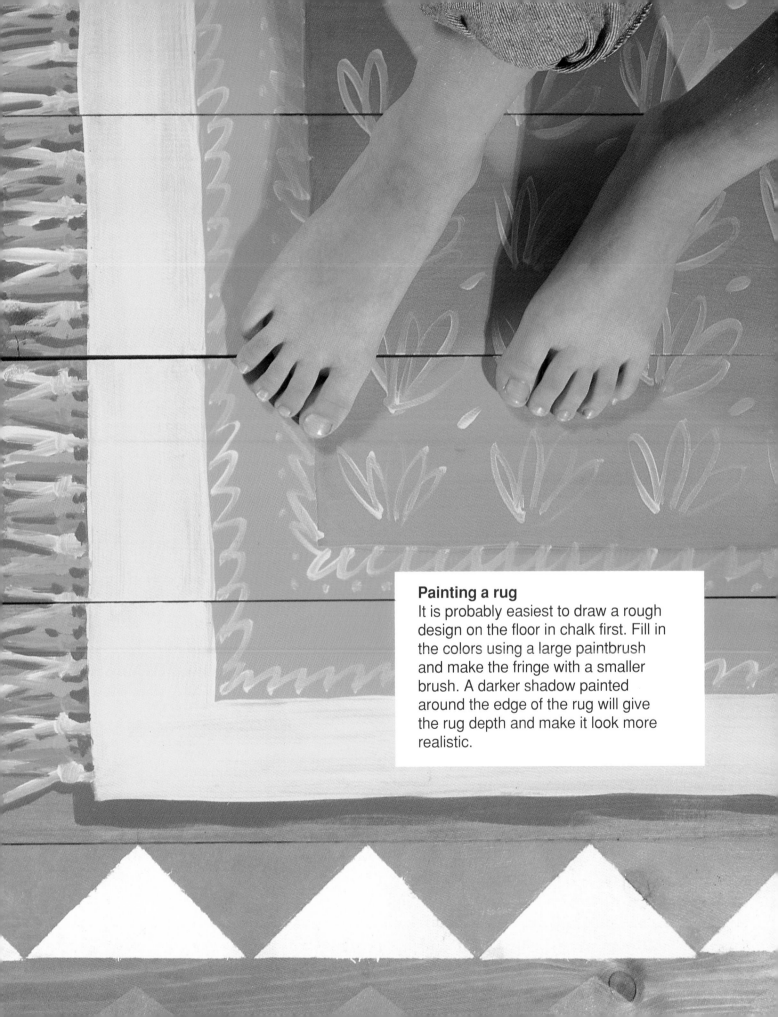

Painting a rug
It is probably easiest to draw a rough design on the floor in chalk first. Fill in the colors using a large paintbrush and make the fringe with a smaller brush. A darker shadow painted around the edge of the rug will give the rug depth and make it look more realistic.

14 Linoleum Tiles

Linoleum makes an extremely practical floor covering because it is so easy to wipe clean. Look for sheets of linoleum or linoleum tiles at builders' supply stores or stores that sell floor coverings. Or ask friends who have just laid a linoleum floor if they have any left over.

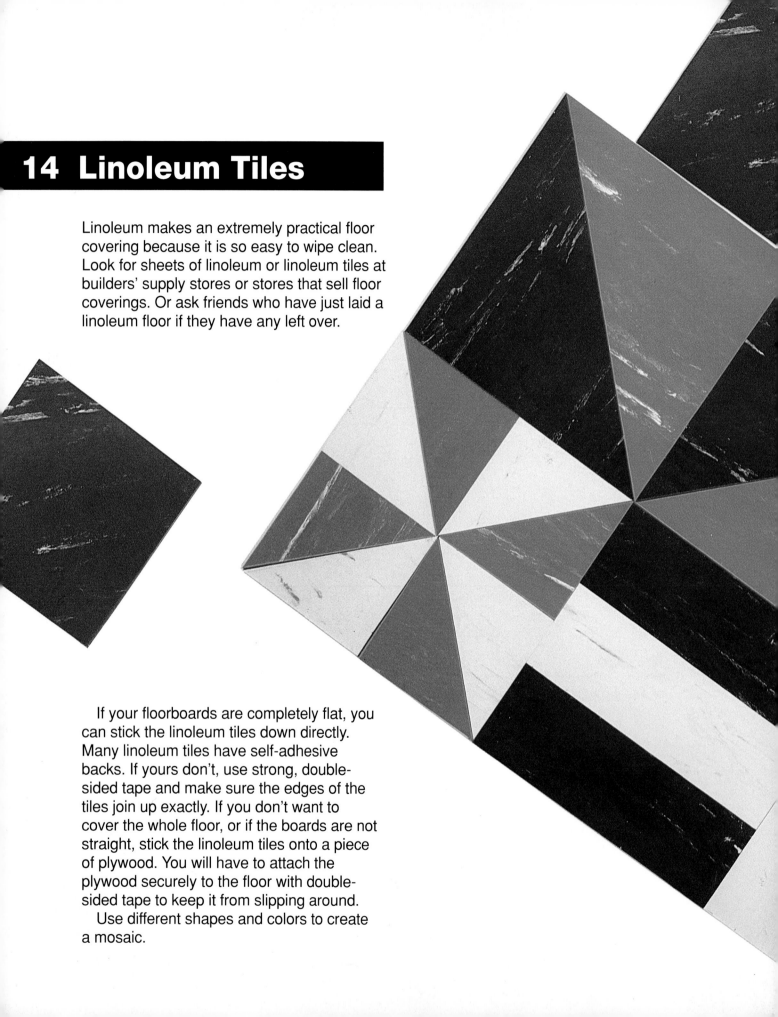

If your floorboards are completely flat, you can stick the linoleum tiles down directly. Many linoleum tiles have self-adhesive backs. If yours don't, use strong, double-sided tape and make sure the edges of the tiles join up exactly. If you don't want to cover the whole floor, or if the boards are not straight, stick the linoleum tiles onto a piece of plywood. You will have to attach the plywood securely to the floor with double-sided tape to keep it from slipping around.

Use different shapes and colors to create a mosaic.

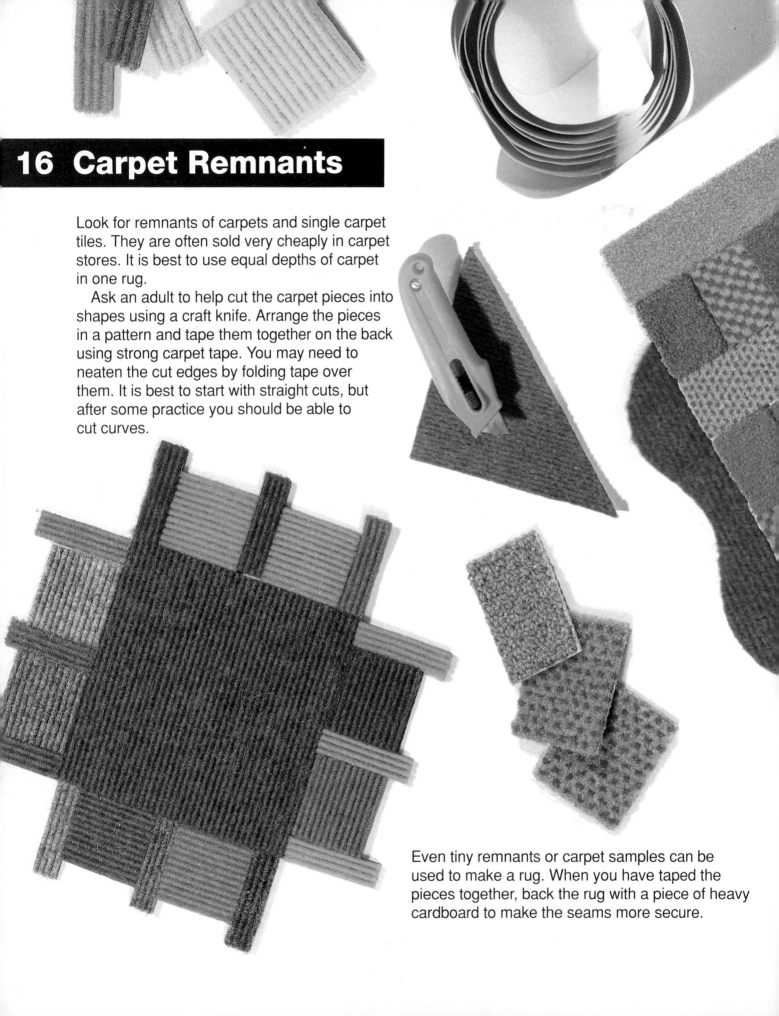

16 Carpet Remnants

Look for remnants of carpets and single carpet tiles. They are often sold very cheaply in carpet stores. It is best to use equal depths of carpet in one rug.

Ask an adult to help cut the carpet pieces into shapes using a craft knife. Arrange the pieces in a pattern and tape them together on the back using strong carpet tape. You may need to neaten the cut edges by folding tape over them. It is best to start with straight cuts, but after some practice you should be able to cut curves.

Even tiny remnants or carpet samples can be used to make a rug. When you have taped the pieces together, back the rug with a piece of heavy cardboard to make the seams more secure.

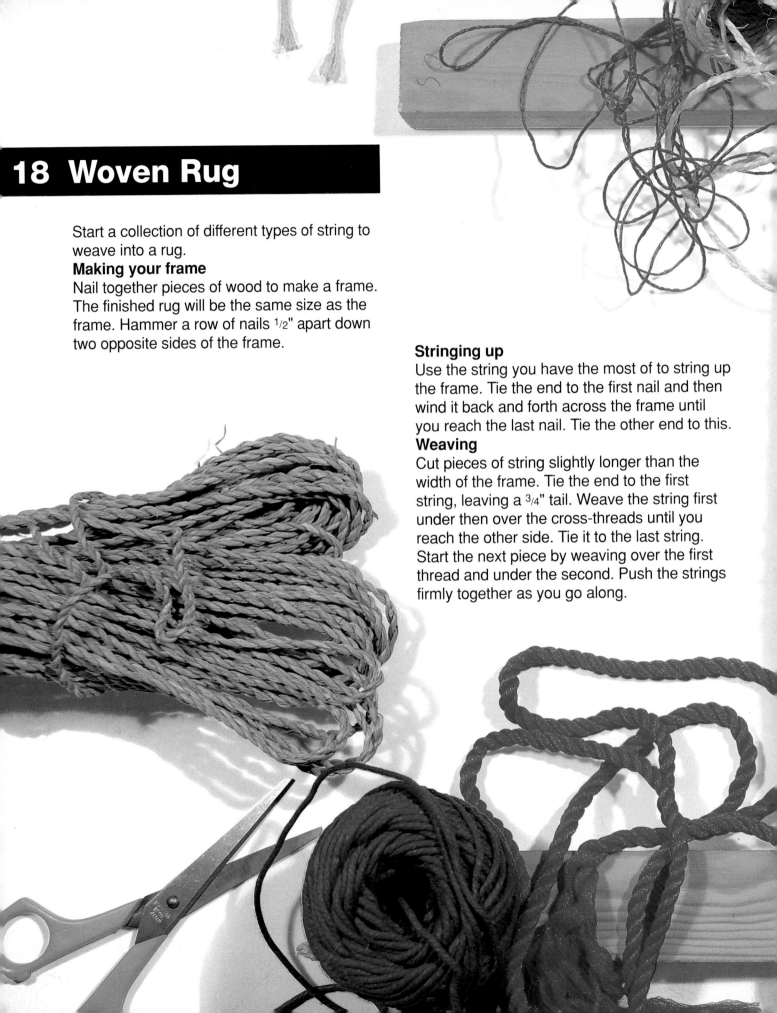

18 Woven Rug

Start a collection of different types of string to weave into a rug.

Making your frame

Nail together pieces of wood to make a frame. The finished rug will be the same size as the frame. Hammer a row of nails 1/2" apart down two opposite sides of the frame.

Stringing up

Use the string you have the most of to string up the frame. Tie the end to the first nail and then wind it back and forth across the frame until you reach the last nail. Tie the other end to this.

Weaving

Cut pieces of string slightly longer than the width of the frame. Tie the end to the first string, leaving a 3/4" tail. Weave the string first under then over the cross-threads until you reach the other side. Tie it to the last string. Start the next piece by weaving over the first thread and under the second. Push the strings firmly together as you go along.

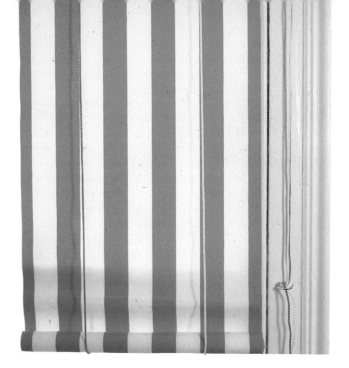

There are all sorts of ways to make window coverings and you don't need to be an expert at sewing.

First measure the width of the window frame. Some fabrics – such as deckchair canvas – come in narrow widths, so you may need to join two or three pieces together.

Remember to ask for permission before putting hooks or nails into the walls to attach blinds or curtains.

Roller Blind

Cut a piece of deckchair canvas slightly longer than your window.

Glue the top around a strip of heavy cardboard. Wrap the bottom around a dowel rod and glue or tack it in position.

Tape two long pieces of cord to the back of the blind at equal distances from the edge.

Nail the top of the blind to the window frame, with the cords dangling behind it. Put two hooks in the wall above the blind directly above the cords. Put a third hook at the top right-hand corner of the window and a fourth at the bottom right-hand corner.

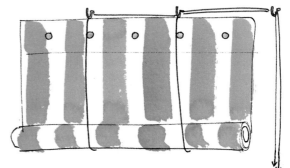

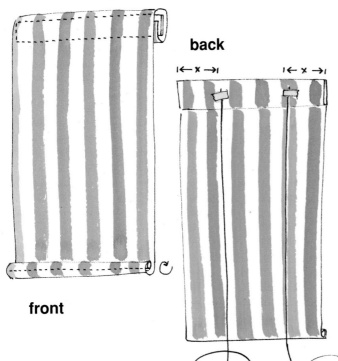

back

front

▶ Bring the left cord up in front of the blind, over the first, second, and third hook, and down to the anchor hook. Bring the right cord up in front of the blind, over the second and third hook, and down. Knot the cords together and wrap them around the anchor hook.

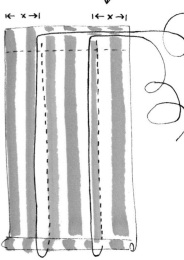

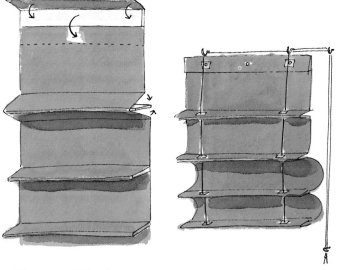

Roman Blind

Cut a piece of deckchair canvas twice as long as your window. Cut a number of strips of cardboard about 2 inches wide and glue them to the material at regular intervals like wedges. Punch holes through the fabric and cardboard. You could decorate the holes with different colored fabric. Thread cord through the holes and attach following the roller blind directions.

Draped Curtain

Ask an adult to cut a broom handle to the width of your window. Screw large hooks into the wall above the window frame to hold the pole in place. You will find it easier if you hammer a nail in first to make a hole. Drape a length of fabric over the pole. It is worth spending some time arranging the fabric so that it looks good.

Plastic Strip Curtain
You can buy heavy plastic strips from a housewares store. Attach one end to a strip of cardboard that is as long as the width of your window. Cut the strips a little longer than your window. Attach the cardboard to the top of the frame. Use ribbons to tie the strips back.

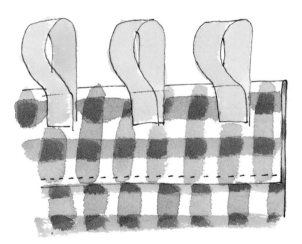

Ribbon Loop Curtain
Make a very simple curtain by turning under the edge of some fabric, gluing it down, and then attaching loops of ribbon.

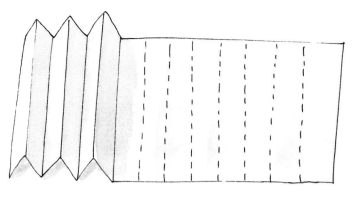

Paper Blind

It may be hard to find a sheet of paper as big as your window, but gluing pieces of paper together works just as well.

Score the paper across the width and make accordian folds. Cut into the folds to make a pattern. You could also cut slits to thread colored ribbon through. Make two holes straight down through the paper for the cords.

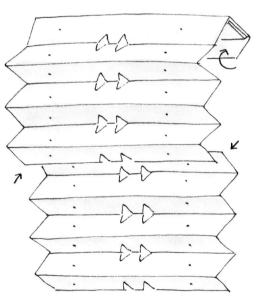

Glue the top and bottom of the blind around a piece of stiff cardboard. Thread a piece of cord through the blind and attach it as for the roller blind. Decorate the ends of the cord with tape.

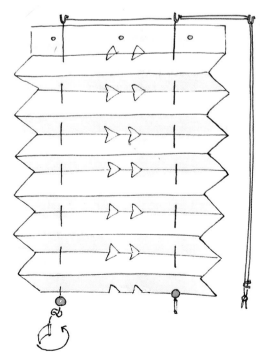

24 Duvet & Cushions

Turn your bedroom into a jungle by painting your own duvet cover. Use fabric paint to brighten up a plain white cover and make some cushions to go with it in coordinating colors and patterns.

Read the instructions on the fabric paints. Most need to be ironed when they are dry. Cotton is the best material on which to paint.

In a simple electrical circuit the positive (+) and negative (−) terminals of a battery are joined by wires to a bulb. A switch is added somewhere in the circuit to turn the current on and off. Ask for advice in any hardware store.

Cardboard Lamp

Cut slits of equal length in the center of two pieces of cardboard – one from the top and one from the bottom – and slot them together. Cut a flap to support the battery and a strip of cardboard to hold it in place. Thread the cardboard through slits A and B in the diagram.

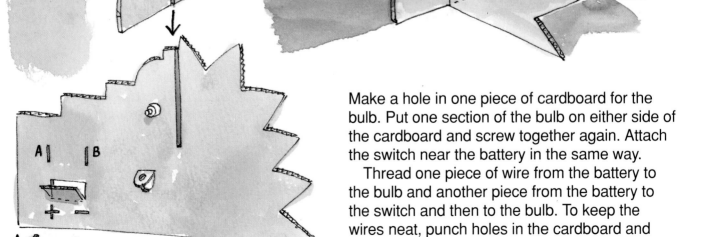

Make a hole in one piece of cardboard for the bulb. Put one section of the bulb on either side of the cardboard and screw together again. Attach the switch near the battery in the same way.

Thread one piece of wire from the battery to the bulb and another piece from the battery to the switch and then to the bulb. To keep the wires neat, punch holes in the cardboard and weave the wires through.

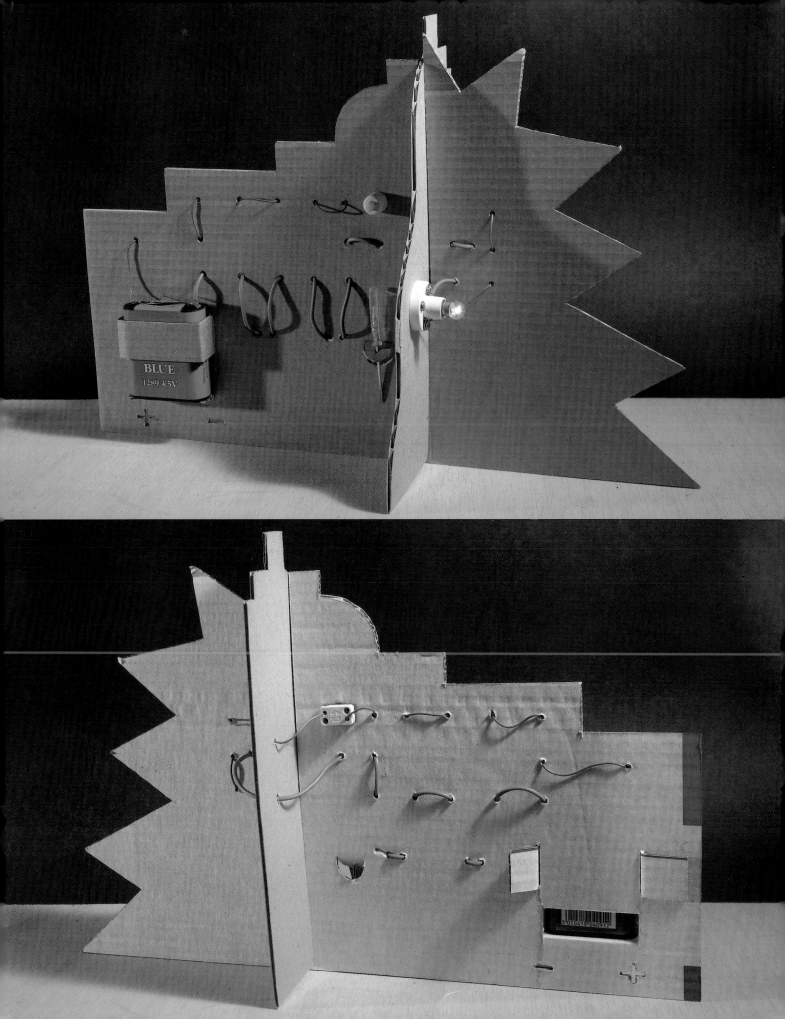

28 Lampshades I

Make a new lampshade from cardboard, fabric, or tissue paper to coordinate with your room. Look around for an old lampshade that you can use as a frame, or make your own from scratch.

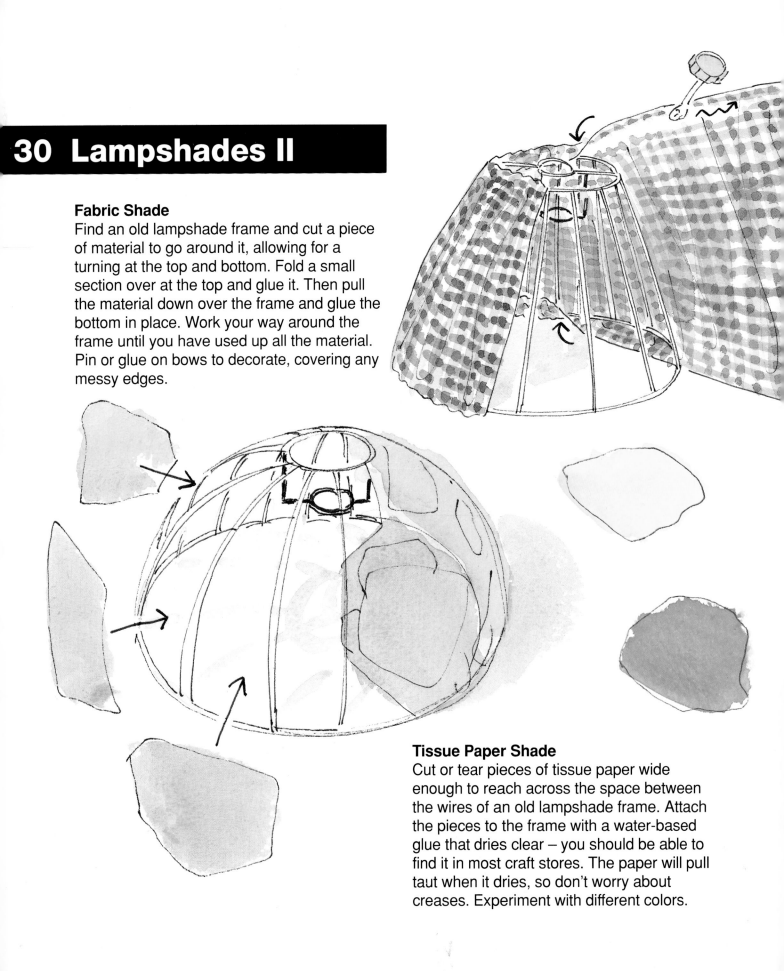

Fabric Shade

Find an old lampshade frame and cut a piece of material to go around it, allowing for a turning at the top and bottom. Fold a small section over at the top and glue it. Then pull the material down over the frame and glue the bottom in place. Work your way around the frame until you have used up all the material. Pin or glue on bows to decorate, covering any messy edges.

Tissue Paper Shade

Cut or tear pieces of tissue paper wide enough to reach across the space between the wires of an old lampshade frame. Attach the pieces to the frame with a water-based glue that dries clear – you should be able to find it in most craft stores. The paper will pull taut when it dries, so don't worry about creases. Experiment with different colors.

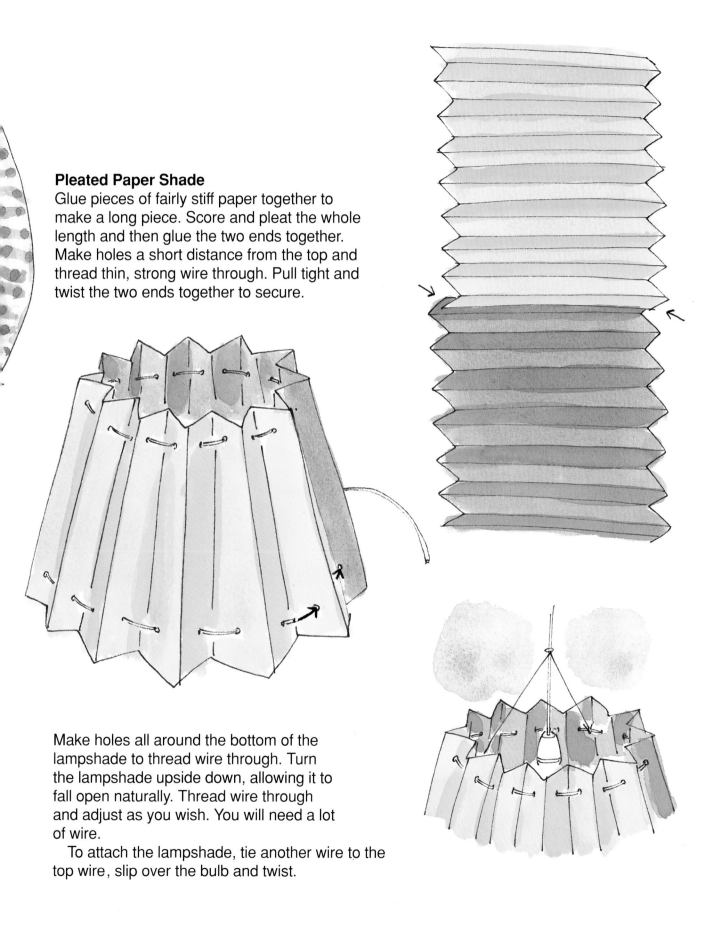

Pleated Paper Shade

Glue pieces of fairly stiff paper together to make a long piece. Score and pleat the whole length and then glue the two ends together. Make holes a short distance from the top and thread thin, strong wire through. Pull tight and twist the two ends together to secure.

Make holes all around the bottom of the lampshade to thread wire through. Turn the lampshade upside down, allowing it to fall open naturally. Thread wire through and adjust as you wish. You will need a lot of wire.

To attach the lampshade, tie another wire to the top wire, slip over the bulb and twist.

Get a mottled effect by sponging one color over another.

You can give old furniture a new lease on life with a coat of paint. Use sandpaper to remove the top layer of paint and make the surface smooth. Use latex semi-gloss paint to repaint the furniture. Try splattering, sponging, or stenciling to give different effects.

Run a brush over a thin surface coat of paint so that the bottom coat shows through.

Cover the area you are working in with newspaper.

Collect old planks of wood or pieces of plywood to make shelves with. Find some bricks to use as supports, or fill old cans with sand or stones. Make sure the supports rest on top of one another and put the shelves against a wall to brace them. Keep your unit low so that it is stable.

You could paint your shelves and supports, or leave them plain if you like the color and texture of the wood.

Collect some cardboard boxes. Most large boxes are made from a layer of corrugated cardboard sandwiched between two flat layers. When the corrugated part has tight folds, the cardboard is firmer and stronger; when the folds are looser, the cardboard is more flexible.

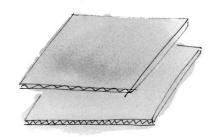

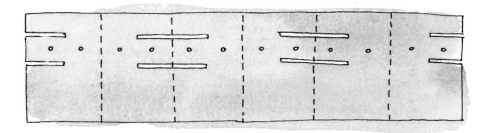

Zigzag Shelves

◀ Score and fold two pieces of cardboard into zigzags. With the cardboard still folded up, cut slits halfway into one side of all the folds. Make sure the slits are in the same place on both pieces of cardboard. Punch two holes through all the layers using a bradawl.

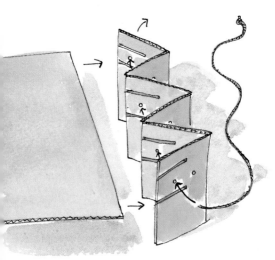

▲ Thread cord through both sets of holes. The back string should be kept shorter than the front string.

Slide a flat piece of cardboard into the slits of both zigzag supports.

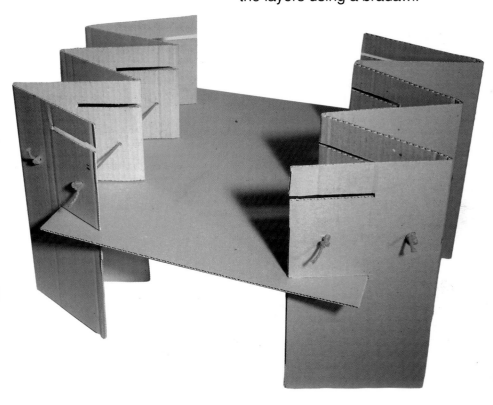

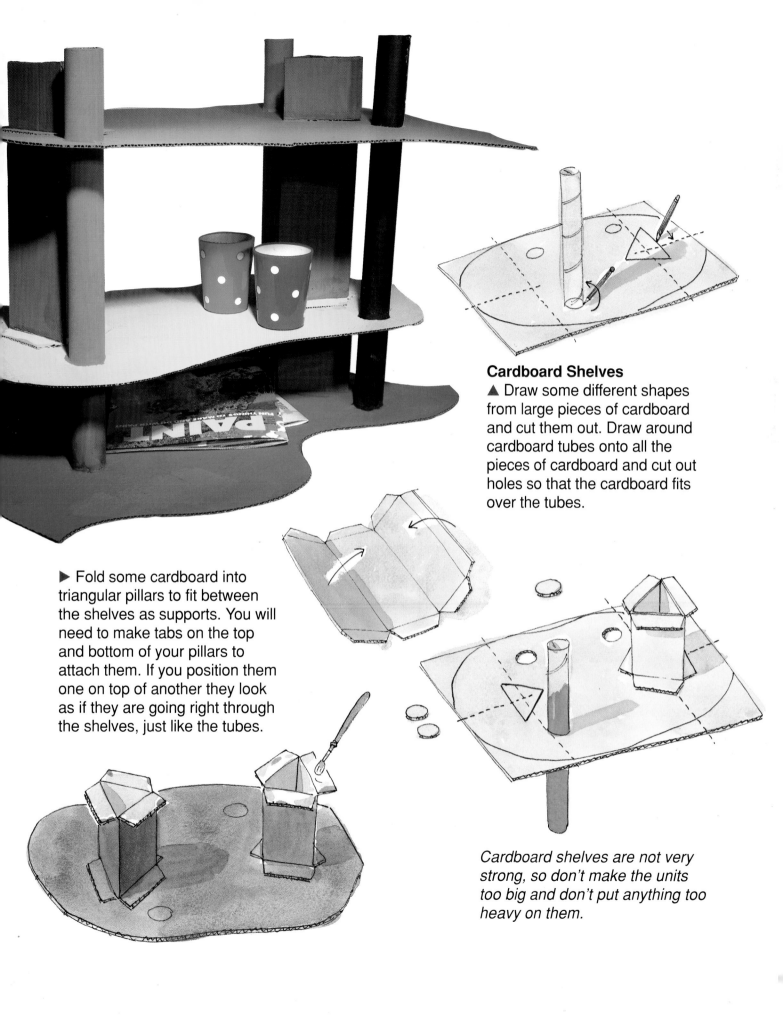

Cardboard Shelves

▲ Draw some different shapes from large pieces of cardboard and cut them out. Draw around cardboard tubes onto all the pieces of cardboard and cut out holes so that the cardboard fits over the tubes.

► Fold some cardboard into triangular pillars to fit between the shelves as supports. You will need to make tabs on the top and bottom of your pillars to attach them. If you position them one on top of another they look as if they are going right through the shelves, just like the tubes.

Cardboard shelves are not very strong, so don't make the units too big and don't put anything too heavy on them.

38 Storage I

Collect different boxes to keep things in. You should be able to find uses for fruit crates, shoe boxes, and even matchboxes.

Moving Table
Find some boards that are the same length or ask an adult to saw some. Use short nails to tack the boards to two pieces of wood placed crosswise.

Screw castors to the bottom of the table so you can move it around.

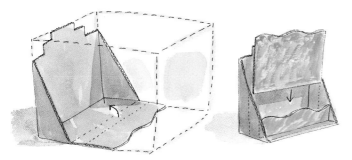

Letter Rack

Cut the top and sides from a cardboard box, leaving a shape like the one in the drawing.

Fold the base back and then up to form the first division of the rack. Slot in more dividers and secure them with strong carpet tape.

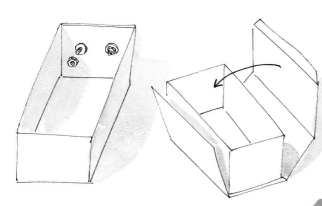

Shoe Boxes

Shoe boxes make good containers for odds and ends. Use nuts, bolts, and washers to screw label holders to the front.

If your shoe box has lost its lid, cut a piece of thin cardboard to fit around it, with an extra flap to glue down. Score the cardboard neatly along the creases and glue in position. Strengthen the front of the box with an extra piece of cardboard.

Use nuts, bolts, and washers as before to attach handles.

Display Shelves

Cut the top part off an old box. Cut a number of strips of cardboard the same depth as the box.

Make slits halfway down the sides of the box and halfway down the strips so that they slot into one another. Cut more slits where one strip crosses another. Use brackets to attach the shelves to the wall.

Use nuts, bolts, and washers to secure the brackets to your shelves. Don't put anything too heavy on the shelves!

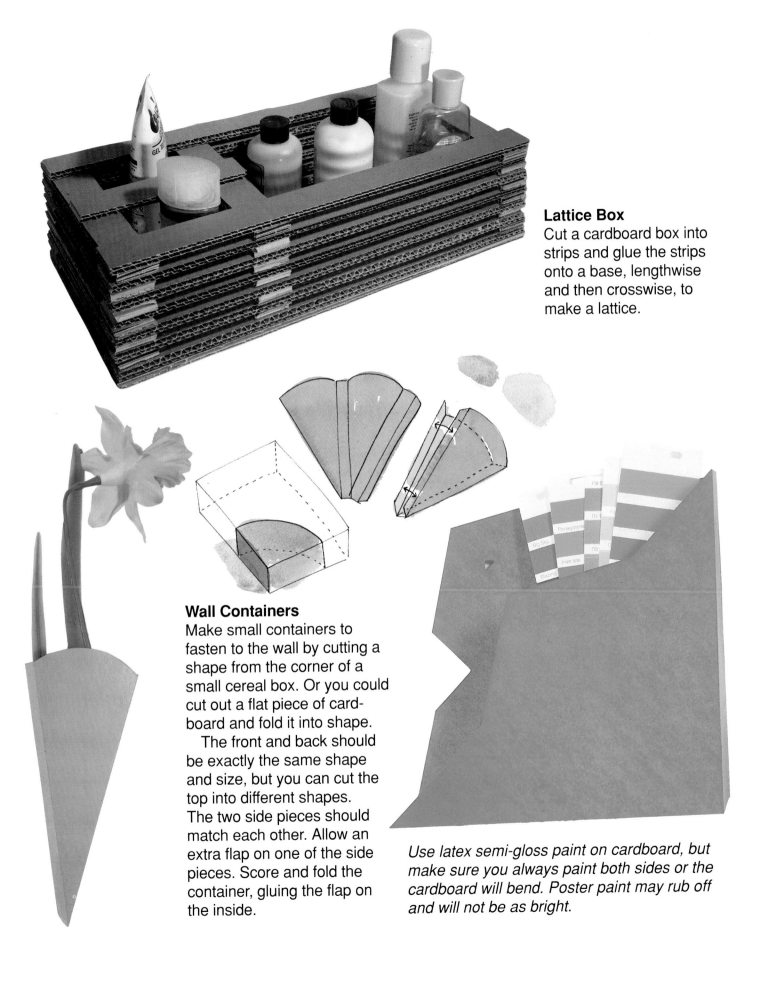

Lattice Box

Cut a cardboard box into strips and glue the strips onto a base, lengthwise and then crosswise, to make a lattice.

Wall Containers

Make small containers to fasten to the wall by cutting a shape from the corner of a small cereal box. Or you could cut out a flat piece of cardboard and fold it into shape.

The front and back should be exactly the same shape and size, but you can cut the top into different shapes. The two side pieces should match each other. Allow an extra flap on one of the side pieces. Score and fold the container, gluing the flap on the inside.

Use latex semi-gloss paint on cardboard, but make sure you always paint both sides or the cardboard will bend. Poster paint may rub off and will not be as bright.

Make a bulletin board to display all your favorite photos, drawings, cards – or whatever you like to collect.

Find a surface that you can stick pins into, such as cork or Styrofoam. You could buy cork tiles and stick them to a cardboard backing sheet.

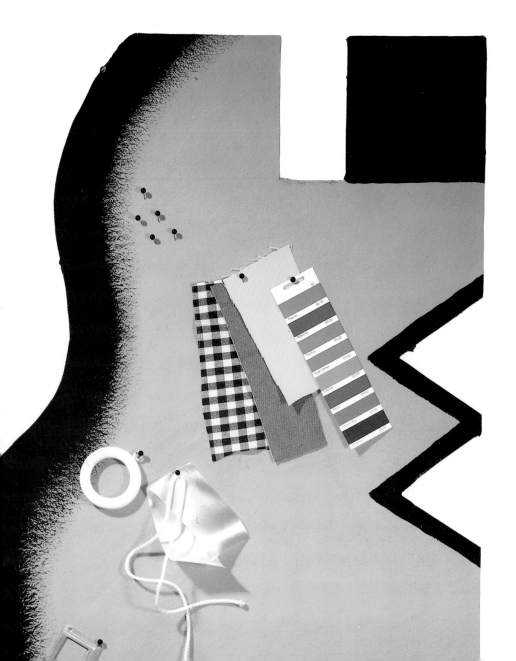

Cut your bulletin board to an interesting shape and paint it or cover it with fabric.

Old picture frames can make good bulletin boards. Paint the frame and backing board. If the backing board is too hard for pins, use removable tape to attach your cards and pictures.

44 Framing

If you have a favorite picture or object, try making a frame for it. Or you may be lucky enough to find a suitable old frame in a junk shop or yard sale that you can renovate.

3-D Picture Frame
Position the object you want to frame on a piece of cardboard. Cut slots in the cardboard where the object touches it. Slot the object into position. Use wedges of cardboard to separate the backing from the front of the frame.

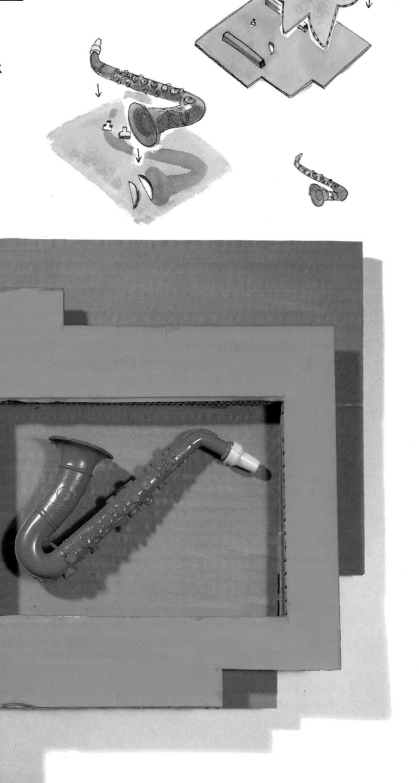

Frame on Frame

Make an existing frame more dramatic by adding more cardboard frames around it. Cut out a piece of cardboard much larger than the existing frame. Then cut a piece from the center, the same size as the frame. Slot the frame into the cardboard. Add more layers of cardboard frames, gradually reducing the size, until the final layer of cardboard is level with the front of the frame. Make sure all the layers fit snugly and then tape at the back.

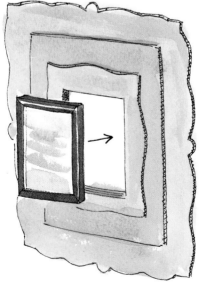

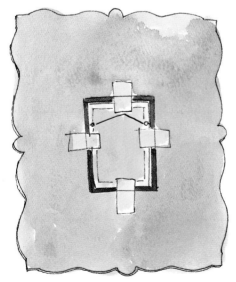

Toolbox

Cut the top off a cardboard box. Make dividers by slotting strips of cardboard into the box.

Cut sloping ends from cardboard to fit inside the box. These pieces should be the same width as the box but about two-thirds taller.

Cut two pieces of cardboard to make the lid for the toolbox. They should rest on the sloping ends and have an extra flap for the handles.

Cut holes for handles but make sure they are not too near the edge or the cardboard may tear.

Attach the lid sections to the base using hinges and nuts and bolts.

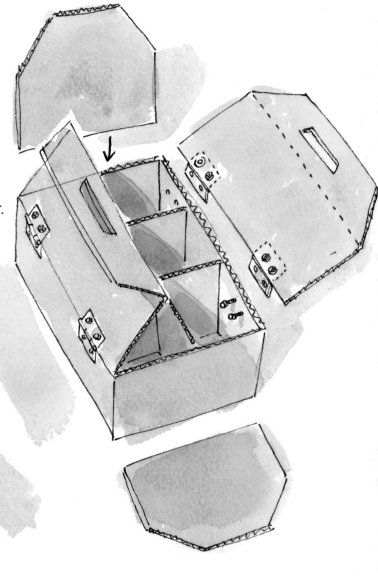

Screen

Collect the largest boxes you can find.
Cut out the sides of the boxes and paint them.
Put the sections of the screen together in a zigzag using hinges and nuts and bolts.

INDEX

First published in the United States in 1994 by
Thomson Learning
115 Fifth Avenue
New York, NY 10003

First published in 1990 by Two-Can Publishing Ltd.
Copyright © 1990 Two-Can Publishing Ltd.

Library of Congress Cataloging-in-Publication Data

Tofts, Hannah
    Do-it-yourself/Hannah Tofts; author, Claire Watts;
    photography, Jon Barnes; cover photography, James Johnson;
    illustration, Kevin Hart.
        p. cm. – (Hands-on)
    "A Two-Can book"
    Includes index.
    ISBN 1-56847-147-5: $16.95
    1. Handicraft – Juvenile literature. 2. Printing – Juvenile
    literature. [1. Printing. 2. Handicraft] I. Watts, Claire.
    II. Barnes, Jon, ill. III. Hart, Kevin, ill. IV. Title.
    V. Series.
    TT160.T53 1994
    745.5–dc20   93-21218

Printed and bound in Hong Kong